Forestry

Written by Jane Drake with Ann Love

Illustrated by Pat Cupples

Kids Can Press

The old fir tree in Cameron's backyard was the best climber in the neighborhood. Cameron and his friends met in the cool shade under its branches. A few years ago, the tree started to lose branches and bark. This spring its needles turned red, the bird family moved to another tree, and Cameron took down his swing.

Cameron's Uncle Erik is a forester. Today he's cutting down the fir. He plans every slice of the chainsaw. First he climbs up the tree, trimming off all the branches. Then, starting from the top, he cuts the tree down in large pieces. Each section thunks to the ground in a shower of sawdust. Cameron is so curious that Erik offers to take him along for a day in the forest.

2

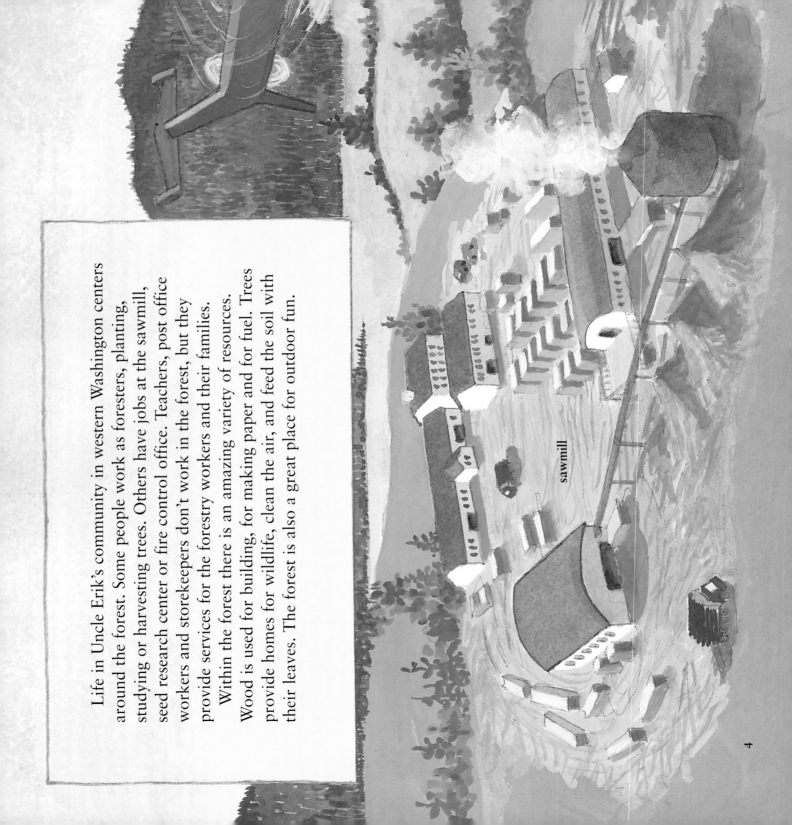

Life in Uncle Erik's community in western Washington centers around the forest. Some people work as foresters, planting, studying or harvesting trees. Others have jobs at the sawmill, seed research center or fire control office. Teachers, post office workers and storekeepers don't work in the forest, but they provide services for the forestry workers and their families.

Within the forest there is an amazing variety of resources. Wood is used for building, for making paper and for fuel. Trees provide homes for wildlife, clean the air, and feed the soil with their leaves. The forest is also a great place for outdoor fun.

sawmill

4

From above, the forest looks like an endless green carpet of trees. But close up, there's much more. Trees are one part of this ecosystem — a natural community where plants and animals live together, sharing space, food, water and air.

The forest is a complicated environment that people must use with care. If trees are cut and not replanted, soil from the forest floor can wash into rivers, choking water creatures. Without the forest to protect them, meadows can become windy wastelands where plants struggle to survive. And the air temperature can rise without the cooling effect of trees. Caring for the forest starts with planning for the future. Most state laws require replanting every tree that is cut within three years. Seedlings should be planted gradually over many years, recreating the natural forest that was cut, with trees of different ages and sizes.

6

Throughout the U.S., each forest has its own variety of trees. For instance, maple, oak, hickory and other trees grow in eastern forests. In the forest where Cameron's uncle works, western species of spruce, fir and pine are common.

Many different kinds of seeds are needed to create the variety of trees that grow in forests. Foresters gather seeds from healthy trees, using tools as simple as jackknives or as fancy as baskets dangling under helicopters. Collected seeds are sorted and sent to nurseries for sprouting.

Some seeds are grown and cared for outdoors. These seedlings must survive all kinds of weather. After three years the young trees are tough enough to live in the harsh conditions of a mountain slope. Other seeds are potted in greenhouses where computers control the temperature, moisture and food. When these seedlings leave the nursery, they are planted outside in their biodegradable pots, complete with good soil and food. It takes at least 50 years for most trees to become fully grown.

Trees are planted in spring or fall, when the ground is moist. Crews, dressed for hard work and lots of bugs, are taken to reforestation areas by truck or helicopter. Most seedlings are planted by hand, using a tool called a dibble. This site has been prepared, so each worker can plant about 100 seedlings in an hour. On rougher ground it takes longer. Machines are used to reforest flat, open areas.

dibble

Many seedlings die in their new environment. Weeds can steal their water, food and light. Insects may damage or kill young trees. To control the weeds and insects, foresters often use chemicals sprayed from planes. Foresters are also looking for environmentally friendly ways to protect the seedlings from pests. At this site, cows are feasting on weeds. Biodegradable tubes protect the seedlings from the nibbling teeth of animals.

11

Look! A forest fire!
They caught this one quickly, Cameron. It's almost out.

Fire control workers are always ready, and they respond immediately to the report of a fire. Planes loaded with foam fire retardant roar down the runway. The foam slows the fire down until ground crews arrive. Winds move fire quickly, so firefighters clear trees and dig trenches ahead of the blaze to stop it from spreading. More planes dump water and dirt until the fire is out. Finally, helicopters equipped with special machines scan for hot spots that might rekindle the fire. Later, foresters will study the burned site to decide what trees to plant there.

Fire is the biggest danger to the forest. In a fire, wildlife is killed or left homeless and valuable wood is destroyed. Lightning starts some forest fires, but most are caused by careless people.

13

Foresters harvest trees like a farm crop. They use aerial photographs, satellite images and computers to help them decide which trees are ready to be cut. Most trees are harvested by clearcutting. That means that every tree in a large area is cut down. Forestry companies prefer to clearcut because it is the cheapest and most efficient way to remove trees. But clearcutting is wasteful. Trees that are too small or the wrong kind of wood are left to rot, and many animals cannot survive the destruction of their forest homes.

14

Harvesting by selective logging removes only specific trees, leaving the rest to grow. This more expensive method is becoming more widely used, especially in U.S. government forests, because it is less harmful to the environment and to wildlife.

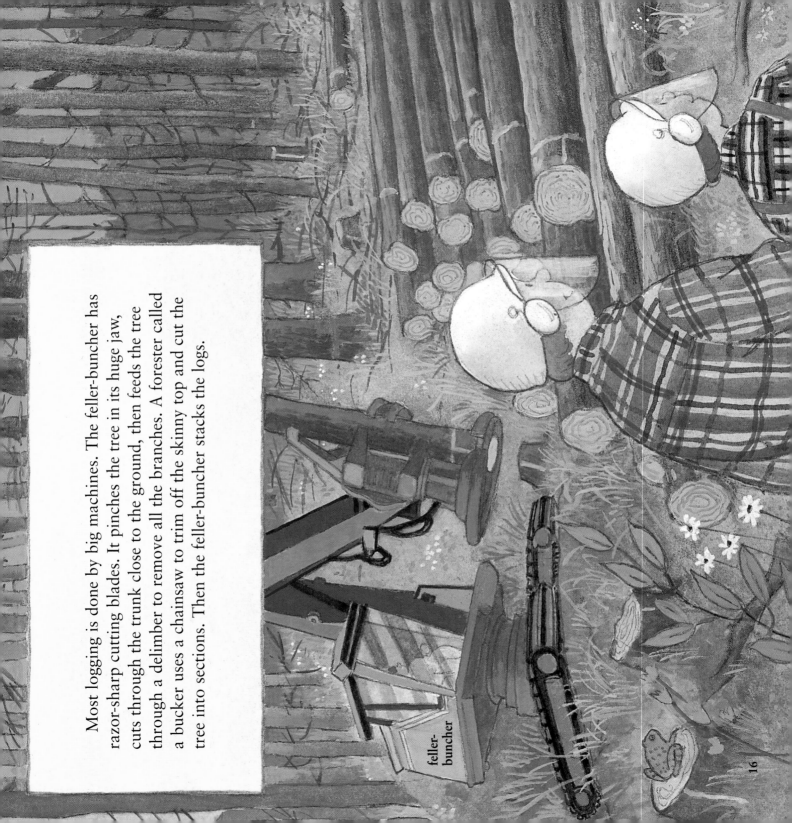

Most logging is done by big machines. The feller-buncher has razor-sharp cutting blades. It pinches the tree in its huge jaw, cuts through the trunk close to the ground, then feeds the tree through a delimber to remove all the branches. A forester called a bucker uses a chainsaw to trim off the skinny top and cut the tree into sections. Then the feller-buncher stacks the logs.

feller-buncher

16

The logs are moved from the cutting site by a skidder. The skidder uses a big claw called a grapple to drag the logs to the road for sorting. Logs used for papermaking go to the pulpmill. Logs used for making wood products, such as furniture, go to the sawmill.

skidder with grapple

17

Tree-markers use detailed maps to help them choose trees for selective harvesting. Bright yellow paint means "cut." These trees are the right size and species and can be easily reached. Red paint signals "leave me alone." These trees have enough space and sunlight and are left to grow for future harvesting, or they are needed for wildlife.

A den tree chart helps the tree-marker save the homes of birds and animals. If a deer herd uses a grove of hemlock for shelter at night, the whole area is protected from logging. Trees close to water hold the soil in place, so they are never cut.

19

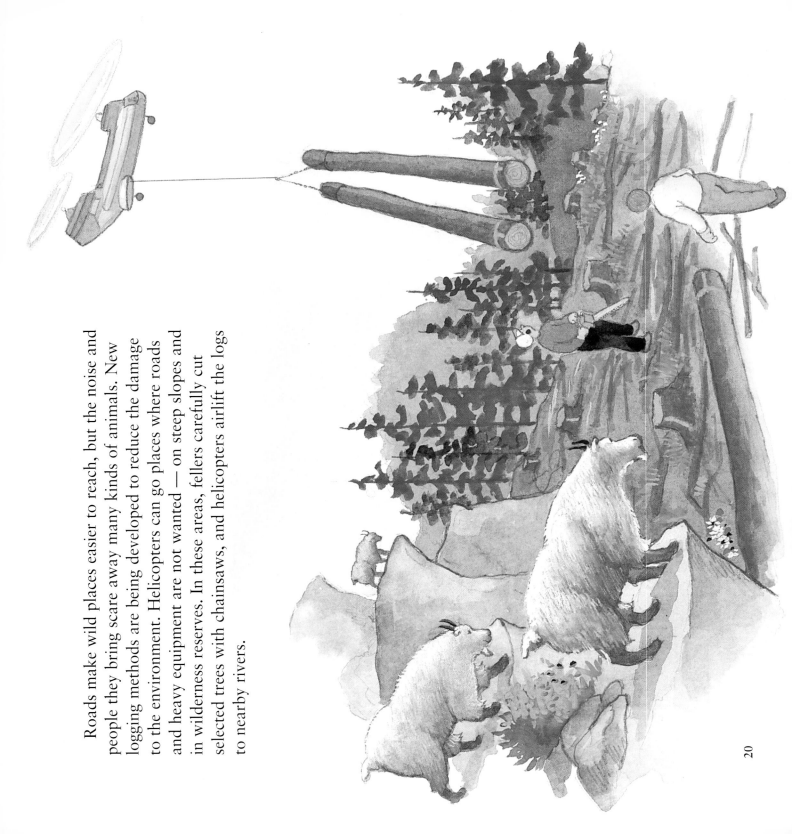

Roads make wild places easier to reach, but the noise and people they bring scare away many kinds of animals. New logging methods are being developed to reduce the damage to the environment. Helicopters can go places where roads and heavy equipment are not wanted — on steep slopes and in wilderness reserves. In these areas, fellers carefully cut selected trees with chainsaws, and helicopters airlift the logs to nearby rivers.

20

The Ecologger looks like a fancy ski lift. Selected trees are cut into logs. These logs are suspended from the Ecologger's cables and carried, above the other trees, to the bottom of the slope.

Logs must travel by water or by road to the mills. On the river, loose logs are rounded up by a crazy-looking vehicle called a boom boat. It scoots between the logs, sorting and shoving them to form enormous log rafts called booms. Booms are often wired together for the trip to the mill. In calm water, tugboats guide the booms.

boom

boom boat

22

Logs that travel by land are loaded onto trucks that rumble down heavy-duty roads to the mills. Logging trucks have many wheels to support the weight of their huge loads.

23

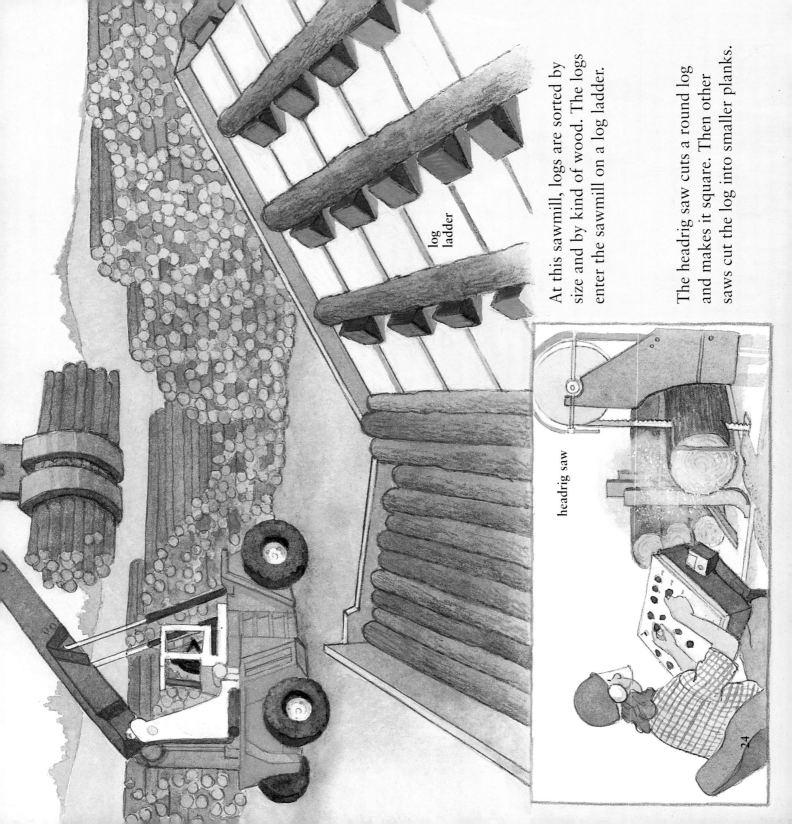

log
ladder

At this sawmill, logs are sorted by size and by kind of wood. The logs enter the sawmill on a log ladder.

headrig saw

The headrig saw cuts a round log and makes it square. Then other saws cut the log into smaller planks.

24

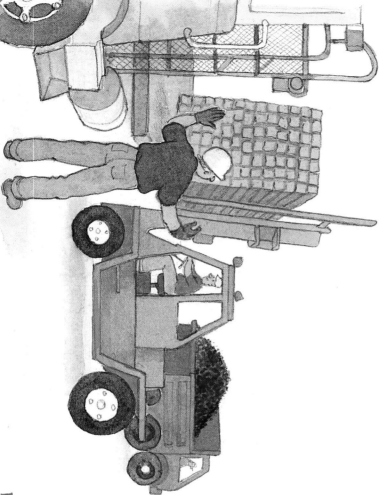

People sort and grade the planks. The best lumber is used to make wood products such as hockey sticks, tables and frames for houses.

Planks are strapped together into bundles, ready for the store or the factory.

No part of the tree is wasted. Bark and scraps are burned to generate energy for the mill or are sold to a pulp and paper company for making paper.

Paper is an important forest product. It is made from wood or recycled paper or a combination of both. This pulpmill uses wood chips, sawdust and recycled paper. They are stewed in a digester with chemicals and water until the mixture becomes very sticky. This gooey concoction, called pulp, is drained on a screen, pressed and dried. The final product is a huge roll of paper that is cut into sheets, boxed and sold.

26

Mills use bleach and other chemicals in papermaking, and these toxins can end up in nearby waterways. Water pollution harms many creatures that live and feed in and around the water. Efforts are being made to reduce pollution by recycling water and using fewer chemicals, but more needs to be done. Everyone can help by recycling and reducing their use of paper products.

digester

27

On the way home, Uncle Erik lands the helicopter near a wilderness park. Enormous old pines stretch into the evening sky. The howl of a wolf makes Cameron shiver. This wild place, with its trees, plants and wildlife, is protected. It will never be used by people for farming, logging, mining or downhill skiing. It will just be there.

While his friends pepper him with questions, Cameron digs holes for two small trees. He has decided on a ponderosa pine and a mountain ash. He chose the pine because it is green all year long, smells good and provides shelter for animals. The mountain ash's orange berries will attract birds. In a few years, they'll both make great climbing trees.

Index

This book is dedicated to Jane Crist — librarian, teacher and friend. — J.D.

The authors gratefully acknowledge the assistance of Ian Barnett; Henry and Kathleen Barnett; Bostock Tree Service; Barbara Cochrane; Crestbrook Forest Industries; Jim, Stephanie, Brian and Madeline Drake; John Dutton; Dr. Robert Edmonds; Carol Green; Rick Greet; Judy Lank; David Love; Wendy Reifel; Kathy Snowden; Kristine Tardiff and Elizabeth Vosburgh. Thanks especially to John McRae for all his valuable help.

Thank you to Valerie Hussey, Ricky Englander and all the people at Kids Can Press. Special thanks to editors Laura Ellis, Lynda Prince and Debbie Rogosin, who know the woods from the trees, and to Pat Cupples, who brought her magic to the illustrations.

First U.S. edition 1998

Text © 1996 Jane Drake and Ann Love
Illustrations © 1996 Pat Cupples

Published in Canada by
Kids Can Press Ltd.
29 Birch Avenue
Toronto, ON M4V 1E2

Published in the U.S. by
Kids Can Press Ltd.
2250 Military Road
Tonawanda, NY 14150

www.kidscanpress.com

The artwork in this book was rendered in watercolor, gouache, graphite and colored pencil on hot-press watercolor paper.

Edited by Debbie Rogosin
Designed by Marie Bartholomew and Karen Powers

Printed in China

The hardcover edition of this book is smyth sewn casebound. The paperback edition of this book is limp sewn with a drawn-on cover.

US 98   0 9 8 7 6 5 4 3 2 1
US PA 02   0 9 8 7 6 5 4 3 2 1

National Library of Canada Cataloguing in Publication Data

Drake, Jane
  Forestry

(America at work)
Includes index.
ISBN 1-55074-462-3 (bound).   ISBN 1-55337-423-1 (pbk.)

1. Forests and forestry — United States — Juvenile literature. I. Love, Ann II. Cupples, Patricia III. Title. IV. Series: America at work (Toronto, Ont.)

SD376.D73 1998   j634.90973   C98-930318-7

Kids Can Press is a **l⊙rus**™ Entertainment company